DECLARE & ESTABLISH

A Guide To Making Declarations

Adrienne S. Young

AY Publishing

Copyright © 2020 Adrienne S. Young

All rights reserved

Except as permitted under the U.S. Copyright Act of 1976, no part of this book may be reproduced, or stored in a retrieval system, or transmitted in any form or by any means, electronic, mechanical, photocopying, recording, or otherwise, without express written permission of the author. The only exception is brief quotes used in reviews. Thank you for your support of the author's rights.

ISBN-13: 978-1-7338264-1-9

Cover design by: Rickie D. Sarratt & Adrienne S. Young
Printed in the United States of America

CONTENTS

Title Page

Copyright

Introduction — 1

Chapter 1 – What to Do When You Get a Word from the Lord — 5

Chapter 2 – Key Elements in Writing Declarations — 9

Chapter 3 – Writing Declarations to Wage Warfare — 13

Chapter 4 - Writing Declarations According to Public Prophetic Words — 16

Chapter 5 - Writing Declarations According to Written Prophetic Words — 19

Chapter 6 - Writing Declarations According to Books — 23

Chapter 7 - Writing Declarations According to Your Word of the Year — 26

Final Instructions — 30

Additonal Tools	33
Acknowledgement	35
Books By This Author	37
About The Author	41

INTRODUCTION

"I need those!" That is what I said to my then business coach as she was making declarations over her business. I asked for her list, and she told me it is imperative that I make my own list. After searching the Scriptures trying to find declarations for my business, I became very frustrated. The concordance wasn't much of a help. During this season in my life, I did not know how to comb through the Scriptures to find biblical principles. So, I decided to just buy prayer books and pray from them about my business. Still, I had the urge to know how to make declarations for every area of my life. Years later, I remember reading a prophetic word from Lana Vawser and thinking, "I need to declare this!" I asked the Holy Spirit how, and He showed me His ways. Then, I asked Him to show me other ways to make declarations from books I was reading, sermons I heard, prophetic words spoken to me, and the rest is history.

What you will read in the following pages, is what I labored over in prayer in desperation to be God's

mouthpiece. Faith comes by hearing and hearing by the word of God (Romans 10:17), and as we make declarations aloud, our faith is grown. We begin to please God because without faith, it is impossible to please Him (Hebrews 11:6)!

As the only creation that can speak, we get to be like God when He created the world with His words. We get to speak into existence what we believe, and as it says over and over in Genesis 1, the New Living Translation, "And then it happened." My prayer is that as you dive into all that God has for you, and as you declare a thing, it will be established to change the trajectory of your life (Job 22:28 NKJV). It is time to declare and establish!

Adrienne S. Young

CHAPTER 1 – WHAT TO DO WHEN YOU GET A WORD FROM THE LORD

Expect God to speak to you. Whether it is through a prophetic word, a dream, a billboard, artwork, in a conversation with a coworker, hearing a sermon or reading a book, God is speaking. It is imperative that we live with the expectation we will hear from the Lord, and what we hear can manifest as we write and speak what we heard. Over the years, I have received many prophetic words and dreams. I prayed for wisdom for what to do while receiving these words and what I should do next to be sure they come to pass. As a result, God gave me a blueprint for the following areas, and without fail, I get to take these words and declare them into being. Now, you will too.

Here's What You Should Do While Receiving Prophecy Publicly:

- Get your cell phone, a friend's cell phone, or a recording device and record what the person is saying.
- If you do not have a recording device, get some-

thing to write with and have someone to take notes for you.
- Stand to receive the word and try your best to remain standing – do NOT fall out.
- Do not allow emotionalism (crying hysterically or wailing) to cause you to miss what is being said; tears may fall, but remain quiet so you can hear.
- Do not speak in tongues while receiving the word unless your Spirit disagrees with it, and you are seeking God to rebuke the word.

Remember, it is important that you hear the prophetice word so that your spirit can soak it in. Let the tears fall and remain standing to receive it.

Here's What You Should Do While Receiving Prophecy Electronically:

- If you receive it via a voice memo, save it immediately.
- Listen to it several times, and in the first few times, listen to it silently.
- After listening to it silently, come into agreement with what agrees with your spirit as you listen to it again by whispering "I receive this," or "It is so," or "I agree, Lord," and give God praise.
- Ask God for clarity if you need it.

- Linger with God after you hear it to see what else the Lord is saying to you; be prepared to take notes or record it on a device.
- Thank God for the person who shared the word with you.

Here's What You Should Do While Receiving Prophecy In Written Form:

- Read it out loud at least three times.
- Read it silently and meditate on a word or phrase.
- Study the Scriptures mentioned for a deeper revelation.
- Highlight, underline, or circle anything that speaks to your spirit.
- Linger with God and allow Him to deposit more into you.

Keep in mind that some prophesies may not manifest for years. Do not lose hope. Every promise in God is yes and amen (2 Corinthians 1:20)!

The Apostle Paul, in 1 Timothy 1:18 (ESV) says "This charge I entrust to you, Timothy, my child, in accordance with *the prophecies previously made* about you, that by them you may *wage the good warfare* (emphasis added)."

This instruction gives us the blueprint for how we are to actualize prophetic words. We are to wage the good warfare, and one way we do this is with our mouths.

As I child, I often played a card game called War, and when it was time to reveal the last few cards, we would say **"I declare war!"** *I prophecy over you, that every time you declare what God has said concerning you, you declare war! God has raised us up with Christ and seated us with Him in the heavenly realm (Ephesians 2:6); therefore, we do not war **for** victory but **from a position of victory!***

We declare war and victory!

CHAPTER 2 – KEY ELEMENTS IN WRITING DECLARATIONS

Job 22:28 NKJV says "You will also declare a thing, and it will be established for you; so light will shine on your ways (emphasis added)."

Although I emphasized prophetic words in chapter one, what I am about to share with you will apply to all areas when it is time to write your declarations. Below is a list of items you will need, and though this may seem elementary to you, I have to give you everything because you are about to write what the Creator of the Universe spoke directly to you, and this is nothing we should take lightly.

ITEMS

- The Declaration Journal, bit.ly/declarejournal, or

a journal of your choosing
- An ink pen (preferably blue ink as this color is associated with the Word of God in the heavenly realm; in the natural, our brain remembers things better when written in color)
- A highlighter as God magnifies a word or phrase to you
- The Bible – try to have at least three translations – you can use the Bible app as well.
- A dictionary: when possible, I prefer Noah Webster 1828 online dictionary; you can use Google as well.
- The recording of the prophecy, a replay video or sermon you received a word from
- The book you want to write declarations from – it does not have to be a "spiritual" one; I have written declarations from books that align with the Word of God.
- The written prophetic word you may have received online
- A quiet space away from any distractions; turn your phone on do not disturb
- Soaking music (optional); one of my favorite artists is Nathaniel Coe III. You can also seach for soaking music on YouTube.

✽ ✽ ✽

Now that you have your items, carve out some uninterrupted time and a sacred space to be with the

Lord. Setting the atmosphere is key. Try not to skip a step if possible. Bind distractions and let anyone in the home with you, or awake when you are, know that you need some time alone with the Lord without interruptions. Sometimes this works for me, many times it does not (inserts laugh). I have learned that when my sons knock on the door, it is a God ordained interruption as they sit with me, observe what is happening, and it becomes a teachable moment.

INTIAL STEPS

1. Turn on your soaking music and sit quietly in the presence of God.
2. Thank the Lord in advance for what He has spoken and what He will speak.
3. Pray in your heavenly language (optional but highly recommended).
4. Ask God for revelation as you write your declarations.
5. Date your journal with the month, day, and year as a record; sometimes what you declare will manifest on the same day a month or a year later.
6. Write the location of the prophecy (if applicable).
7. Write who God spoke the word through – this is not for their glory; when the word manifests, you can share it with the person to build up their faith to continue prophesying.

Now you will learn how to write your declarations according to various categories. This list is not an exhaustive one, but it covers the major areas. Let's get started.

CHAPTER 3 – WRITING DECLARATIONS TO WAGE WARFARE

Now that you have received a word, you have your materials, and your atmosphere is ready, it is time to write your declarations. Remember, when you declare a thing, it shall be established. When kings in the Bible made a decree, it became law and could not be reversed (see Daniel 2 and 6 and Esther 3). When we decree the Word, God watches over his Word to perform it (Jeremiah 1:12).

"For My thoughts are not your thoughts, neither are your ways My ways, says the Lord. For as the heavens are higher than the earth, so are My ways higher than your ways and My thoughts than your thoughts. For as the rain and snow come down from the heavens, and return not there again, but water the earth and make it bring forth and sprout, that it may give seed to the sower and bread to the eater, So shall My word be that goes forth out of My mouth: it shall not return to Me void [without pro-

ducing any effect, useless], but it shall accomplish that which I please and purpose, and it shall prosper in the thing for which I sent it." Isaiah 55:8-11 AMP

Again, do not get weary as your declarations may take days, weeks, months and even years to manifest. Keep declaring and wage the good warfare!

The number one thing I do when writing declarations is to

write them in presence tense.

I believe in calling those things that are not as though they are and not what they will be. I write declarations in first person presence tense, and other times I feel led to write them in third person presence tense. The same goes for when I declare out loud. I may say them in first or third person depending on what Holy Spirit leads me to do. Always be led by the Holy Spirit as He knows all things! (1 Corinthians 2:10)

Here is a list of areas that you can make declarations in. This is not an exhaustive list, but a good start.

- Marriage
- Health
- Finances
- Career

- Relationships
- Business
- Children
- Ministry
- Desiring a child
- Desiring a spouse
- Desiring a home
- To combat depression
- To combat anxiety
- To close a deal
- To have favor
- To experience God deeper

❈ ❈ ❈

Now, it is your turn. Take a minute and write out declarations based on one of the areas in the above list, from a sermon or a passage of scripture you've been meditating on recently.

CHAPTER 4 - WRITING DECLARATIONS ACCORDING TO PUBLIC PROPHETIC WORDS

The best way I can help you with this method is to use an example from a word given to me in 2018 at a conference about running into the new year. The apostle used phrases and Scriptures that I turned into declarations. Remember, the key is to write in present tense and look at different versions of Scripture to declare. He preached about Joseph being shackled (Psalm 105:18) and having beautiful feet (Romans 10:14-15). You will see exclamation points on declarations that sparked excitement for me. That is my preference, as I like to declare with different intonations in my voice. If you agree with any declarations below, declare them!

❊ ❊ ❊

- I'm running into 2018! I'm not slowing down!

- God has released an anointing on my feet, and I will run into my destiny.
- God has put prosperity in my feet.
- My feet are delivered from every shackle and fetter.
- I run again, dance again, and leap again into what God has for me!
- I'm going where God has told me to go!
- What the enemy meant for evil, God is turning it around for my good!
- Every curse sent against my life is turned into a blessing.
- All things work together for my good because I'm called by God. I'm called according to his purpose.
- Every hurt, every pain, and every disappointment in my life turns for my good.
- I believe God for miracles in my feet.
- I will not leave this year in shackles, in bondage or in pain in the name of Jesus.
- God is bringing me to a gate called beautiful, and my feet gain strength as I behold the beauty of the Lord.
- God causes me to go places I've never seen before.
- God is sending me to unusual places of ministry.
- God is causing my feet to travel even to nations I've dreamed about (I listed nations here).
- I get ready for that opened door. I get ready for the Macedonian call.
- I'm ready for the divine connections.
- I'm ready for the finances I need to go where God

is sending me!

- The fire of God is back in my feet! I do not leave 2017 broken and hurt. I am going into 2018 with fire, passion, anointing, and grace in the name of Jesus.
- 2018 is a year of beauty and glory for me where I behold the beauty of God, and my feet are restored.

❋ ❋ ❋

Now, it is your turn. Take a minute and write out a few declarations based off a prophetic word you've received either publicly or electronically.

CHAPTER 5 - WRITING DECLARATIONS ACCORDING TO WRITTEN PROPHETIC WORDS

If you follow me on social media, you know I follow Lana Vawser and have made many declarations out of her written prophetic words shared on Facebook and her website. I print out the prophecy as I like to highlight or underline what I want to declare. Now, you could declare straight from the printout if you prefer. For me, the more I see it, write it, and say it, the more it is engrained in my spirit. Here's an excerpt of a prophetic word for writers in 2018, and I wrote declarations after each paragraph as an example. These declarations are still applicable today, and if you are a writer, declare them!

❋ ❋ ❋

"Writers, you are called to write. You are called to pen the words the Lord gives you. The battle has been over your pen, and the distractions have come in this season of transition, but there is a heralding taking place in the heavenlies."

I am called to write. I am called to pen the words the Lord gives me. I come against distractions in this season of transition. There is a heralding taking place in the heavenlies!

✣ ✣ ✣

"You aren't moving into a season of visitation and encounter that looks like anything you have experienced before. This is a completely new season and the enemy has been fighting hard to keep you from this place, because you are not only going to see Jesus and encounter His heart and the supernatural realm in ways you never have, you are going to experience a whole new level of empowerment of the Spirit of God upon your writing."

I am moving into a season of visitation and encounter that doesn't look like anything I have experienced before. This is a new season for me, and the enemy can no longer keep me from this place. I see Jesus and encounter His heart and the supernatural realm in ways I never have. I experience a whole new level of empowerment of the Spirit of God upon my writing!

✣ ✣ ✣

"The Lord is going to PEN more through you in this season than you have experienced before. There are going to be things that the Lord will release to you in this season to PEN that is going to be MAJOR KEYS of breakthrough for many individuals, for cities and nations."

The Lord is penning more through me in this season than I have experienced before. The Lord is releasing things to me in this season to pen major keys of breakthrough for many individuals, cities and nations.

❊ ❊ ❊

"The Lord showed me that in this new season of visitation and encounter that not only is the scribe anointing significantly increasing upon your life, but the Lord is going to teaching you to understand the language of the Spirit in greater ways, to move in the realm of the Spirit with greater wisdom and discernment and to understand by the revelation of the Lord greater secrets of His heart."

In this new season of visitation and encounter, the scribe anointing significantly increases upon my life. The Lord is teaching me to understand the language of the Spirit in greater ways, to move in the realm of the Spirit with greater wisdom and discernment and to understand by the revelation of the Lord greater secrets of His heart.

* * *

I heard the Lord decree over the writers:

"I AM COMING LIKE I HAVE NEVER COME BEFORE AND TO RELEASE WHAT HAS NEVER BEEN RELEASED THROUGH YOU BEFORE. NEW WINE IS BEING RELEASED"

The Lord decrees over me, His writer, "I AM COMING LIKE I HAVE NEVER COME BEFORE AND TO RELEASE WHAT HAS NEVER BEEN RELEASED THROUGH YOU BEFORE. NEW WINE IS BEING RELEASED" So it is, and it is so!

* * *

Now, it is your turn. Take a minute and write declarations based on a prophetic written word. If you need one, check out www.lanavawser.com.

CHAPTER 6 - WRITING DECLARATIONS ACCORDING TO BOOKS

This year I am captivated by the book Faith & The Marketplace by Bill Winston. I read it through once and am rereading it again one chapter a day to write declarations from it. Here is a brief example of how you can take a paragraph from a book, including the introduction in this case, and create declarations.

❈ ❈ ❈

"As Matthew 11:19 says, "God's wisdom...is shown to be true by its results" (Good News Translation). God strategically positions us in the marketplace to not only bring His compassion but also, through our work performance, demonstrate His wisdom and ultimately His influence."

As Matthew 11:19 says, "God's wisdom...is shown to be

true by its results." God strategically positions Adrienne Young in the marketplace to not only bring His compassion but also, through her work performance, demonstrate His wisdom and ultimately His influence.

* * *

"In these last of the "Last Days," according to the Scriptures, we will experience an outpouring of God's wisdom and witness explosive inventions that can only be compared with God's original Creation. And this outpouring will come through the Church, the Body of Christ. It will not be the intellectual, technological, or scientific wisdom taught at universities. It will be the wisdom that only the Holy Spirit teaches. It's the wisdom that established Daniel to counsel the Babylonian government, and Joseph to bring forth the most powerful economy the world had ever seen, which brought them both to prominence and marketplace leadership."

In these last of the "Last Days," according to the Scriptures, I experience an outpouring of God's wisdom and witness explosive inventions that can only be compared with God's original Creation. This outpouring comes through the Body of Christ, of which I am a part. I operate in the wisdom that only the Holy Spirit teaches and not the intellectual, technological, or scientific wisdom taught at universities. I have the same wisdom that established Daniel to counsel the Babylonian government, and Joseph to bring forth the most powerful economy the world had ever seen, which brought them both to prominence and marketplace leadership. I have access to this same wisdom as God has a storehouse of it waiting on me (Proverbs 2:7-8).

❋ ❋ ❋

Now, it is your turn. Take a minute and write out declarations based off a portion of a book you have read or are currently reading that is speaking to your spirit for a current situation.

CHAPTER 7 - WRITING DECLARATIONS ACCORDING TO YOUR WORD OF THE YEAR

I wrote a blog in 2018 about how God led me to take my word of the year and make declarations according to it. This method is what I have used ever since that day, and I have seen manifestations of it quickly. If you do not have a word for the year, seek God for it now; even if this is the middle or end of the year, the Lord can still give you a word.

Here Are Some Ways You Can Make Declarations Of Your Word Of The Year.

1. Write the definitions of your word. I prefer Noah's Webster's 1828 dictionary and a Google search: "define comfort."
2. Write the synonyms.
3. Write the antonyms.
4. Take it a step further by writing down the defin-

itions of two to three synonyms that speak to you.
5. Do a word search for Scriptures that line up with your word. In the Bible app, search for it or look in a concordance.
6. Find a song that has your word in it and write out the lyrics.

Once you have completed the steps above, write your declarations OR you can just declare from what you have written. For the antonyms, you will declare against them.

The key is not to limit God in the area He wants you to decree in. For me, he had me to write "In my marriage, I ____; in my ministry, I ____, and in my business, I ___" (fill in your word declaration).

✣ ✣ ✣

WORD OF THE YEAR: COMFORT

1. Noah Webster: To strengthen; to invigorate; to cheer or enliven. To strengthen the mind when depressed or enfeebled; to console; to give new vigor to the spirits; to cheer, or relieve from depression, or trouble. Amenity: the quality of being pleasing or agreeable in the situation, prospect, disposition, etc.
2. Synonyms: rest, enjoyment, pleasure, relaxation, relief, quiet, amenity, etc.

3. Antonyms: discontent, displeasure, lack, upset, worry

Declarations Based on the Word Comfort

- In my life, marriage, business, and ministry, I am strengthened. I am invigorated. I am cheerful.
- I speak to depression and declare my mind to be renewed.
- I am consoled by the Holy Spirit.
- I have new vigor!
- I am relieved from depression and trouble.
- I am comforted.
- I have rest, enjoyment, pleasure, relaxation, relief, quiet, and amenity.
- I have the quality of being pleasing and am agreeable in situations and in my disposition.
- I come against discontent. I am content in every state that I am in (Philippians 4:11).
- I come again displeasure. I come against lack because the Lord is my shepherd, and I shall not lack (Psalm 23:1 NIV).
- When I face situations, I am not upset; I am calm. I do not worry because the word says to be anxious for nothing (Philippians 4:6-7).
- Even though I walk through the darkest valley, I will fear no evil, for God is with me; his rod and his staff, they comfort me (Psalm 23:4).

* * *

Now, it is your turn. Take a minute and write out declarations based on your word for the year. If you do not have one, seek God. If you keep hearing, or have heard a word repeated, consider using that word as well. For instance, in our 2019 Warriors United Conference, we heard the word "catapult" several times. Do not limit God in how He chooses to speak and write declarations from it!

FINAL INSTRUCTIONS

God formed the world by speaking it into existence. We are made in the image and the likeness of God giving us the same authority. No other living creature can speak words but us. Let that sit with you. The Creator of the Universe chose us to be like Him. Therefore, we have the ability to create with our words just as He did. What a mighty God we serve!

After declaring, sit with God on what you are to do; seek the Lord for any instruction and action steps to do next as faith without works is dead.

To get the declarations in your spirit more, voice record them. Insert pauses between phrases to repeat after them; consider adding soaking music to the recording by playing it in the background as you declare. Play the declarations on a commute or in the evening before bed. The more you hear them, the more you declare them, the more your faith and your expectation will increase for God to bring them to pass.

There is not a perfect way to write declarations.

You do not have to do everything outlined in this book. Use it as a *guide*, and seek the Holy Spirit on His ways for you. My prayer is that you will see what you say. Keep declaring a thing, and it will be established for you!

---

[1] https://lanavawser.com/2018/10/03/writers-there-is-a-heralding-taking-place-in-the-heavenlies-a-new-season-of-visitation-and-encounter/

[2] *Faith & The Marketplace,* pg. 15

ADDITONAL TOOLS

In addition to making declarations, learning more about prayer, specifically intercessory prayer, is essential to my spiritual journey. Go to my YouTube channel to access a free two-hour webinar. From there, you can get information to enroll in our online 6-week intercessory prayer training where you learn about:

Week 1 - The Call, Heart and Commitment of an Intercessor
Week 2 - The List Intercessor
Week 3 - The Personal Intercessor
Week 4 - The Crisis Intercessor
Week 5 - The Warfare Intercessor
Week 6 - The Prophetic Intercessor

ACKNOWLEDGEMENT

Thank you to my amazing husband who allows me to spend time with Jesus every morning to declare. Thank you to my sons who knock on my door and slide beside me to hear and see what I am doing. Thank you to my Business Besties, Otesia and Roshanda, who pray for me and sharpen me. Thank you to my brother who helped me design the cover. Thank you to my Remnant Sisters and my family who always support me. Thank you Holy Spirit for teaching me all things. Let's continue to build together for the Kingdom of God!

BOOKS BY THIS AUTHOR

Don't Go Thrifting Without Me: A Mini Guide To Maximize The Benefits Of Thrifting

Do you have a desire for high fashion looks, but lack the budget to shop in expensive stores? Are you interested in redecorating your home, but need to find great pieces for low prices? Do you simply love the excitement of a great deal?

If you answered yes, "Don't Go Thrifting Without Me," an Amazon bestseller in fashion, art, and home decor, is THE book for you! Packed full of years of shopping tips and inside secrets of the trade, this debut release by Adrienne S. Young demystifies the process of thrifting while highlighting all of the benefits.

Covering topics from what you should wear, to when you should shop, Adrienne gives step by step practical advice to thrift any look or transform any room! Learn directly from this gifted Thrifting Queen and other popular thrifters she's brought

along to share their best kept secrets! Get ready to expand your wardrobe and upcycle your home's style!

Women Who War: Wives Warring For Their Marriage

Do you believe God ordained your marriage, and the enemy has done everything he can to destroy it? Have you wanted to give up and walk away from it all? Are you tired of fighting and want to know strategies on how to war? If you answered yes, "Women Who War" is THE book for you!

When the cops arrived at my home, I knew the enemy had launched an all-out attack against my marriage, and God taught me how to war.

Covering wives from the Bible and stories from modern-day women who war, let's journey to their battlefields where you hear their stories and receive strategies to war such as:

- Declarations to speak over your marriage
- Scriptures to meditate on
- How to uncover the real enemy
- Prayers to pray

Get ready to train and become a wife who wars!

ABOUT THE AUTHOR

Adrienne S. Young

Known for her real, radical, and relevant style of delivery, global corporations partner with Adrienne for her expertise as an Image and Retail Brand Strategist.

She is the founder of the nonprofit Remnant Warriors Global, Inc. and Women Who War which helps women and girls know how powerful they are in God and to walk in their kingdom authority.

Whether she is strategizing in the boardroom, giving captivating keynote speeches, or ministering the Word, any encounter with Adrienne will inspire you to be present in your purpose.

Originally from Gaffney, SC, Adrienne and Eddie live in Fort Mill, SC with their two sons. They enjoy football, board games, and watching classic shows together.

Made in the USA
Monee, IL
29 June 2020

35152024R00026